ALSO BY PETER GIZZI

The Outernationale

Some Values of Landscape and Weather

Artificial Heart

Periplum

THRESHOLD SONGS

Threshold Songs

PETER GIZZI

Wesleyan University Press

MIDDLETOWN, CONNECTICUT

WESLEYAN POETRY Wesleyan University Press
Middletown CT 06459 www.wesleyan.edu/wespress
© 2011 Peter Gizzi ALL RIGHTS RESERVED
Manufactured in the United States of America

Wesleyan University Press is a member of the
Green Press Initiative. The paper used in this book meets
their minimum requirement for recycled paper.

Library of Congress Cataloging-in-Publication Data
Gizzi, Peter.
Threshold songs / Peter Gizzi.
p. cm.—(Wesleyan poetry)
ISBN 978-0-8195-7174-8 (cloth : alk. paper)—
ISBN 978-0-8195-7175-5 (ebk.)
I. Title.
PS3557.I94T47 2011
811'.54—dc22 2011005648

5 4 3 2 1

Frontispiece: Robert Seydel, *Untitled* [Starry Hare],
2008. Mixed media collage. Courtesy of the Estate of
Robert Seydel. Photograph by Stephen Petegorsky

This project is supported in part by an award
from the National Endowment for the Arts

NATIONAL
ENDOWMENT
FOR THE ARTS
A great nation
deserves great art.

*

for Robert, for Mother, for Mike

called back

A voice comes to one in the dark. Imagine.

SAMUEL BECKETT

THRESHOLD SONGS

The Growing Edge

There is a spike
in the air
a distant thrum
you call singing
and how many nights
this giganto, torn
tuned, I wonder if
you hear me
I mean I talk
to myself through you
hectoring air
you're out there
tonight and so am I
for as long as
I remember
I talk to the air
what is it
to be tough
what ever
do you mean
how mistaken
can I be, how
did I miss it
as I do entirely
and admit very

well then
I know nothing
of the world
can see it now
can really see
there is a spike
a distant thrum
to the empty
o'clock autumn litter
it's ominous, gratuitous
the asphalt quality
these feelings
it's Sunday in deep space
and in the breeze
scatters, felt presences
behind the hole
in the day, sparks
ominous spike
I've not been here
before, my voice is
looking for a door
this offing light
reaching into maw
what does it mean
to enter that room
the last time
I remembered it
an *un* gathering

every piece of
open sky into it
the deep chill
inventing, and
is it comfort
the cold returning
now clear and
crystalline cold
I standing
feet on the ground
not under it
I frozen and
I can feel it
to meet incumbent
death we carry
within us a body
frozen ground
what does it mean
to be tough
or to write a poem
I mean the whole
vortex of home
buckling inside
a deep sea whine
flash lightning
birth storms
weather of pale
blinding life

Lullaby

Everyone's listening to someone in the air

and singing knows every chestnut from way out when

the mourning dawn of living each apple and every atom

in the tooth actually small circuits uncover vast spaces

even if invisible you see the picture field and the lightning

is there a difference between a photograph of a child

and what memorials what or what is the role of art if any

within your particular emotion machine

the limits of thought and seeing perhaps

it explains water is one way to apprehend air

the morning light is in us

a stinging charge in the mouth

this is something everyone feels at least once

here before you started listening to the song

at the beach and soldiers by a desert

if anybody looked we are all stranded by the shore of something

I mean to say seeing pictures inside as they are

Hypostasis & New Year

For why am I afraid to sing
the fundamental shape of awe
should I now begin to sing the silvered back of
    the winter willow spear
the sparkling agate blue
would this blade and this sky free me to speak
    intransitive lack—

the vowels themselves free

Of what am I afraid
of what lies in back of me of day
these stars scattered as far as the I
what world and wherefore
will it shake free
why now in the mind of an afternoon is a daisy
    for a while
flagrant and alive

Then what of night
of hours' unpredicated bad luck and the rot
    it clings to
fathomless on the far side in winter dark

Hey shadow world when a thing comes back
comes back unseen but felt and no longer itself
    what then
what silver world mirrors tarnished lenses
what fortune what fate
and the forms not themselves but only itself the sky
by water and wind shaken
I am born in silvered dark

Of what am I to see these things between myself
    and nothing
between the curtain and the stain
between the hypostatic scenes of breathing
and becoming the thing I see
are they not the same

Things don't look good on the street today
beside a tower in a rusting lot
one is a condition the other mystery
even this afternoon light so kind and nourishing
a towering absence vibrating air

Shake and I see pots from old shake
    and I see cities anew
I see robes shake I see desert
I see the farthing in us all the ghost of day

the day inside night as tones decay
    and border air
it is the old songs and the present wind I sing
and say I love the unknown sound in a word

Mother where from did you leave me on the sleeve
    of a dying word
of impish laughter in the midst my joy
I compel and confess open form
my cracked hinged picture doubled

I can't remember now if I made a pact with the devil
    when I was young
when I was high
on a sidewalk I hear "buy a sweatshirt?" and think
buy a shirt from the sweat of children
    hell
I'm just taking a walk in the sun in a poem
    and this sound
caught in the most recent coup

Eclogues

This clock entitled, simply, my life, speaks at irregular intervals
so loud there isn't room for a boy.

Few celebrate the interval inside the tock

others merely repeat fog. The unhappening of day. The sudden
storm over the house, the sudden

houses revealed in cloud cover. Snow upon the land.

This land untitled so much for soldiers, untitled so far from swans.

Sing. Flag. Boy. Idyll. Gong.

Fate disrupts the open field into housing starts, into futurities
neglected corners and mites.

This again, the emptied anthem, dusty antlers, pilsner flattened.

To do the time, undo the Times for whom?

Bells swinging. The head rings no. No.

The space inside is vast.

The prayer between electrons proportionately vast.

The ancestry between air and everything is alive and all is
alpha everywhere

atoms stirring, nesting, dying out, reforged elsewhere,
the genealogist said.

A chromosome has 26 letters, a gene just 4. One is a nation.
The other a poem.

Eye of the Poem

I come to it at an edge
morphed and hobbled,
still morphing. There is also
the blowtorch grammar's
unconquered flame.
That may sound laughable
but we'll need strength.
We'll need the willow's flex,
the flapping windsock.
We'll need every bit
of solar wind, serious goggles.

This is the snow channel
and it's snowing. Hey,
you wanted throttle,
you wanted full bore.
Stay open to adventure.
Being awake is finally
a comprehensive joy.
Stay open to that nimbus
around the back porch reverie,
every parti-colored aura
on cars left and to the right of you.

Ascending through the core
I am silly with clarity.
Born of air I am and
the dappled buttresses
in this vacuum glisten.
I remake my life.
What pressure animating giddy coil.
What not the flutter, every
ting and flange calling to you.
A bright patch over the roof
on the jobsite singing itself.

Snow Globe

This house is older than the lilac trusses glistening
    in winter ice,
older than the pack of Winstons on the wire chair,
older than the chair as well as this glass of water
    holding water. Is it older?
The house lurks under the sky, which has stood over it.
A time when this patch was a field, deer maybe shat in it,
    grazed a few leaves from a sprig, now fallen.
The house is covered in fresh snowfall, lovely
    in reflected mercury light,
its weary glow damaging to the cardinal flirting
    between branches
of a stalled ornamental maple. Where is my head
    in this data? All this
indexical nomenclature. It's not reassuring to know
    the names tonight, lousy and grigri and non.
Just words to fill space older than a house, a bird,
    this glass and my hand.

How I Remember Certain Fields
of Inquiry (and ones I only imagine)

To feel it. A draft
from a room opening
next to the head.
A prism lit momently
and by its glow
I know me. It
plays through me. It
at the back of me.
Plato wasn't wrong
shadowing me.

Analemma

That I came back to live
in the region both
my parents died into
that I will die into
if I have nothing else
I have this and
it's not morbid
to think this way
to see things in time
to understand I'll be gone
that the future is already
some where
I'm in that somewhere
and what of it
it's ok to see these things
to be the way they are
I can be them
have been them
will be there, soon
I know why I came here
to be back here
where my parents went
I know that I'll be there
to join them soon

it's ok to think this way
why shouldn't I
whose gonna say I shouldn't
a doctor, some friend
I have no wife in this
at night, late, the dark
myself at the ceiling
the arguments continue
I'm with it, it's with me
I am *quelque chose*
something with birds in it
a storm high above Albany
I am ghost brain I
sister to all things cruelty
the mouse-back gray
of every afternoon
and your sorrowing
now that you're gone
and I'm here or now
that you're here and
I'm gone or now
that you're gone and
I'm gone what
did we learn
what did we take
from that oh
always dilating

now that you're here
and also gone
I am just learning
that threshold
and changing light
a leafy-shaped blue
drifting above
an upstate New York
Mohican light
a tungsten light
boxcar lights
an oaken table-rapping
archival light
burnt over, shaking

Fragment

When you wake to brick outside the window

when you accept this handmade world

when you see yourself inside and accept its picture

when you feel the planet spin, accelerate, make dust
    of everything beneath your bed

when you say I want to live and the light that breaks
    is an inward light

when you feel speed of days, speed of light

if one could fancy vision then let it be of you

let it be thought breaking in your view

★

This Trip Around the
Sun Is Expensive

Shipboard is
what winter is

what isinglass
moonlit wave
winter is

Winter surf
all time booming

all time viscous air
not black, night
winter dark blooming

surfs of winter ice

No time away
from igloo ice

Winterreise
hubba hubba like

This trip
around the sun
is expensive

To work
the proud flesh

Wound bright

Shipboard is
what winter is

what isinglass
moonlit wave
winter is

Winter surf
all time booming

all time viscous air
not black, night
winter dark blooming

surfs of winter ice

Gray Sail

If I were a boat
I would probably roll over
If I were a prayer

If I were a beech stave
Beech bark
If I were a book

I would sing in streets
Alone in traffic

If I had a gown
I could be heroic
With a flowering mane

If I had a boat
I would eat a sandwich
In broad dazed light

I would come visit
As a holy book
If I were a boat
If I had a prayer

On Prayer Rugs and a
Small History of Portraiture

If water were to boy as boy is to bird then swim in air
the folktale might go.

This day opens a keepsake. Closing and opening
unlike a keepsake

the face in the portrait is still no longer itself
a dusty satellite

decaying in its orbit around my polarfleece.

★

I am angry today, that the face, the trans-
missions the being alive not being

is so easy to imagine or why there is a grain to the voice

a striation in blackness calling, gnarled and
throbbing like . . .

★

I awake to like

to light on grass, the ungoverned sheen of grass lit
out this window the day is

gorgeous. The day is thrilling in the good old sense of that word
when the world sat by the fire. The fire is

raging, has raged, was raging.

★

The figure in green blossoms too next to every rotting blade,
every bleating sow, bird de-

caying with an aroma of green, word transmogrophy-
ing green, the mint

in the flame, the heat of
the brain expiring steam, steaming thought

and the piles stacked archival thinking pyre.
This is the drudge of fire.

★

I am alive today, yes alive not being alive

being with the lost ones and the living lost within the lost hours
lost faces lost who find

tendrils of smoke and shoots bursting forth in rain, from rage
raining wavering bursting sight

this way and that plume this day
that day. Where was I?

★

Every day a portrait. Every day a point. A pirouette
into aught

awe, off-centered asymmetrical lighting
alive in contrast, alive

to contest. Away in itself in itself a way out of here

of transport panning the scene or skein of sight
the syncroflash of being sparrow.

★

Wholly exhausted sparrow poor little sparrow
of figured time

conferenced addressed flattened beatified fallen
to my knees

forgive my indulgence calling you
on the carpet by the bookcase, this figure

all the time falling forgiving not
forgotten.

A "Buddy Poppy" for Mike

words lines face
feign trace strange

rain pain end
the sun

the sun

Undersong

When the bottom drops out of August

when the bottom drops and the summer disc burns deep in its bed

when nerves sing, blaze, and flame their circuit

when the bottom of August sticks out

and clouds above change shape

when bodies inside spin and change shape

the bottom falls and meaning peeks out with chagrin

the hot skin of August no longer sending messages of summer

birds no longer at rest

when the winds pick up and the cool air is just behind it all

the bottom of the news story reveals itself

the story is cold

Pinocchio's Gnosis

The season folds into itself, cuts a notch in me. I become thinner. My heart splinters and a wooden sound invades the song, interrupts my ire. Today the planet is mostly dirt, mostly water—forget about my lyre. And if you look close everywhere coming to the surface, bare trees, bare yard showing through.

★

The wind is blowing west. The wind leaning, the trees sway, the clouds there. Grief is an undersong, it has its region naturally like a river valley spilling over like a nest inside the inside of feeling. Roughed. Go west originally came from ghost stories and not the campfire kind but a real ghost and a real story bleeding.

★

In my father's house I killed a cricket with an old sole. Funny how being dead troubles the word. I am trying to untie this sentence, to untidy the rooms where we live. No words in the soup, no soup in this sky, no more history written onto onionskin, peeling onion skins.

★

If I decide to laugh all the time I'll surely rid myself of tears. Why accept less than a joke, teasing lone from the lonely, bending the guy into guidebook. Hey you, Mr. *Sacer interpresque deorum*, how about a good bray, a laugh track in sync with your lyre? No?

★

Tears too form a roaring truth on the rolling green. Sure it's a nice day. A splendid day when joy met doom, the entire forest wept. Is not the tree more beautiful than the wood, the crown more lovely than the grain? There is an order. Small things assert themselves.

★

Once we understood velvet suggested elegance and distinction or my ruddy cheeks were more chevalier than clown or sawdust, din and clatter, tin cymbal. But today you have no joy for yesterday's plaything. Sumptuous velvet has lost its bloom. The rider is now that "funny man," his ceaseless chatter.

★

All the world's a stooge. The secret and silent world worn from abuse and those surfaces abrading imagination. The patient world of the abandoned daydream so gay and corrosive. We have entered the semantics of useless things.

★

I am trying to untie the anvil sitting on my head I call my heart. This is a new sensation. I mean sing song bang bang behind my eyes. You've heard this rhyme before.

★

In came a fisherman, he wanted a bride, we held up a seal and gave him a stamp, then hit him with a sickle, let go a little spittle, threw him off a bridge, then peed on the wall. With a magical broom, the wind sang sweep, like an oar in air we ascend. We power the instrument and apply a salve, uncover the ghost behind *fig*. Mistake it for an omen then quiet the cloud, the cloud just there seen through a cataract. We wallow in shallow, stick to the surfeit, singularly tremble, are immune to sting. We consult the leaves and measure the air.

★

It was a simple mallet. It spoke simply, whammo, blam, I understood perfectly. Its oscillations filled the dark in waves of blue, some green and felt like no other mallet in my life. Its use was not significant only its shape, after all it was a tool.

★

Sunday, the silver of asphodel will not save me. If only I were rich. I could write "happiness."

★

If Monday a whole world begins, if to build a flower, if naked at the base of a sycamore, if animated camouflaged bark, if a tear in front of a weather-swept lens, or if laughter at the banquet-crazy table, if eyes opening an ingenious fire, if only to paint this ray only.

★

I had been working the mine for scraps of dust. Head bent for years. When I came up the years had gone. The world was not the world and children were whizzing past me now, with blurred exuberance and CGI forcefulness. What to do as the boards rotted and gave. The paint peeled, macadam lumpy.

★

What is a man but a papered miscellany, a bio furnace blowing coal, a waste treatment plant manufacturing bluster, an open signal full of seawater, a dark stranger turning over the dark next to you.

★

Friday ends in a burning shack. A humpback oratorio spewing roses. The swashbuckler enters from the right singing his pantaloons off. The glint off his sword performs a vast speech, the torch inside an idea, pinwheel sparks squealing on the commons, simply exhaustion after a long day with small children. Hats airborne.

★

This body only lasts for so many days. It's got a shelf life. It's got time-lapse, time-based carbon life. There's you and it and now you are it. That's the paradigm. Dream and enter this evolutionary atmosphere, highly susceptible to laws of gravity, entropy, falling at a startling velocity. Flying is out or so significantly not the same as to be pretty much out.

★

It wasn't meant to be this way. Let me do this now. I don't want to do it again. Let it be said I made an attempt to give relief to the dark. It didn't work. Won't work. Don't really want it to work. It's hard to say. Old as the world itself, war toy and doll, born from necessity to do grown-up work. To slumber in a dark full of memory and figure, to yellow on shelves in catalogs, to become a fit subject for a poem. To be classified, mistakenly, for always.

★

Dreams are such a solid state and then porous and then heavy wet air evaporating, you know: the Blue Fairy walked the bridge-rail over concrete gardens, below her cars and cows packed tightly, sliding, screeching before waking into the sparkling air of modern poetry.

★

And so the singer cast a shadow. It was like every other shadow and so we were comforted. The song was summer itself. Green and a special blue went into all of us. We sat and sweated in our chairs. It wasn't exactly pretty when the song, the green and blue, went into our heads.

★

In chairs we continue the odd alignment of earth in its bearings, the dirt inside bread, spinning and adjusting our breath. But enough of the singer and the special song of summer. We were tired of you, grew tired of these greens and blues, tired of the ray's long sad decline. It bent way down and didn't feel special anymore.

★

It wasn't meant to be this way, the wind leaning, the trees sway, the stars there. Take the long walk home past shadows, alleys, and culverts past streets in midnight past footsteps out there. Take the long walk take the verdigris the periwinkle above it the soot and sirens and odd laughter in the park. Take the promise and transform the man. Look hard into the air.

The shadow cast a singer. It was like every other shadow and so we were comforted. But who would stay the same even if the ray's report is the same. I am changing and you know about this too. The fuzz haloed with heat lines in a cartoon. I am summer the shadow the song and the solstice. Green and a special blue went into all of us.

Basement Song

Out of the deep
I dreamt the mother.

How deep the mother
deep the basement

the body, odor of laundry
the soul of a bug.

The grass inside
the song stains me.

The mother stains me.
That was the year

they cut my throat
and toads bloomed

on my voice box.
I have kept my head up.

Have kept myself
out of trouble

but deep is trouble
deep is mother.

Deep the song
inside summer.

Did I tell you it hurt
accepting air in a new body?

And since the change
the air burns.

★

Tiny Blast

Just a small song with a dash of spite.
A tiny thistle below the belt.

That's it, you know,
the twinge inside this fabulous cerulean.

Don't back away. Turtle into it
with your little force.

The steady one wins this enterprise.
This bingo shouter. This bridge of sighs.

And now that you're here be brave.
Be everyway alive.

A Ghost Card for Robert

What do you see when you see a dress sounding in deep indigo, a head made of text, a paper halo torn about the head.

★

What do you see when you see the shape of a hare and a galaxy, a river and some rushes, when you see the outline of hare and its positive adrift.

★

What do you see when you read from left to right, a cartoon boy on a cartoon lawn, arms outstretched, when you see the word SUN in block capitals over there, a shaft of whiteout above the hare leaping into an inked heart into a ghost boy into a green ray into space.

★

You'll see the red and blue shift, you'll see orbiting patterns, and now you see a woman buried in sepia with child.

★

There is also a yellow star of construction paper and, on it, a handwritten plus or a sign, the number 2 in red ink, illustrations.

★

And what do you see when you see anatomical tubes spilling paint into diaphanous patterns becoming a page becoming a book, a wry smile, a dead man, a spectacled creature and silver temples, a scuffing of smoke above a magical head.

Moonlight & Old Lace

And when I died
I entered a moonlit canvas
from the late 19th century.
There am I
blinking in greens, violets.
At first a giggling mirage
of dusk and paint.
Joy came upon me.
A corona of moths
in white oil about me.
A Japanese lantern.
But after a fashion
which when you're dead
is an eternity I begin
to settle into painterliness
and the grace vivant
of moonlit brushstrokes
and the true depth
of that moonlight.
Silver and old lace
and its relation to music
listing at nature's mirror.

But the empty center
of whitish marks
its indelible air
arctic and sharp
whizzes through me.
I am no more
alive than canvas.
No more dead than alive.
Whose wind errs forth?
What ungainly measure
unwinds underfoot?
Speak world
glower and burn
and illumine your fancy
these moments rouse.
I know there is a distant
world ahead.

Tradition & the Indivisible Talent

If all the world says something
we think then we know something
don't we? And then the blank screen
or memory again. You crazy.
No, you crazy. It's like this
but almost always
when time-lapsed words
and weather-swept flowering trees
move in empathetic wind.
I am rooted but alive.
I am flowering and dying.
I am you the wind says, the wind.

The embiggened afternoon
was just getting started
and to be adrift and stuck
can be a pleasant sensation
like loving abstraction
or a particular object's nimbus.
Pick one and look at it,
human or digital, vegetable,
mineral, alive or dying,
it's all atomic anyhow

much closer, the electron
part of being. Being,
it's a small word.
After all absence makes
the particles move faster.
The path tilted up to the right
and the angled view
so dramatic in boisterous sun.

When a thought's thingness
begins to move, to become
unmoored and you ride
the current with your head,
feel yourself lift off like
birdsong caught in the inner ear
even the curios seem animated
in their dusty shelves—
the song is alive.
That part of tradition.

Birdsong and daybreak,
are they not the same at the root?
Twigs torn from brambles
nest and house this cooing thing.
Close your eyes. The notes
imprint their solar magic homing

a musical refrain built out
in a sculptural vortex—
the applause of rushes
sung into a larger sequence.
The sky. And now the word is fire,
fire in the heart, fire in the head.
Fire above and fire in bed—
seemingly the only element
to get gilded up in song.

How about dirt? I love you
like dirt. I miss you dirty mouth,
dirty smile, oh, and my dirt
is your dirt is nice also.
Closer to the ground, perhaps,
on the ground, that's real enough
and those goddamn spuggies
are fledged and it's spring
and the books in my shelves
in my head have all turned. Nothing
but earth and peat and mold
and rich soft living manna
you can breathe. The must
at the root of it all, desire
and wanting, must know.

Springtime in Rutledge

I don't know from pinwheels

I am far from boots and their fabulous parade, from tubas

what happened to me was god in small things

and flying on the ground it's funny to be here

next to the shadow you left behind

the river keeps time with nothing

nowadays just little blasts of air

and when I say river I don't mean river

do you see the ribbon inside space and time

it's a kind of river, a kind of nothing cascading above

and that's how it is

tiny lights at a county fair sending you a telegram

Lullaby

All animals like to nuzzle with their soft parts

what of it when you see the leafy conflagration in spring

a reminiscing eventual in small wistful bursts

the rhythm of sweeping

everything orbiting in this path

the daytime moon and the mourning dove

both are gray and still with us

even today what is soft and has depth is pleasant

Saturday can be like this too alone in the garage

the organic symphony encircling

the furrowed lanes of mint and clover

remember this and breathe deeply when you can

A Penny for the Old Guy

Everything's the same just faster.

An unusual amount of fracture, office worker, and eclipse.

Time wigging into amperes about me.

An unusual collar starched and pulled taut over the skin.

The genetic text has become real touching me, touching down.

Are we not born of inequity, property, loot, grandeur, flinty grammar?

Are we not bread-like, soft tissue, heat-seeking, and fragile?

In a room of heady effort tomorrow is indeed a fabulous sail billowing.

Any porous room billowing may be feathered and lined with French verse cobbled from the vender's brute cries.

Not a jeering mass at mardi gras but telepathy.

The joker skull of yesteryear has opened a door, fortress dust, human dust.

Tranquil snow-globe dust blanketing evenly, softly.

And now that the things for jack are coming to an end, I'm a nursery rug away from naptime.

Here on the other side, the water grasses waving, deep under.

Apocrypha

Wisdom is a kindly spirit but does it love me? And righteousness? There's nothing in it.

1. To poetry I leave my senses, my deregulation, custodial duties, and to be a janitor is a great consolation.

2. It gave me my mother back through all her years.

3. To love these children, so full of neurons and consciousness. What joy to clean up and put a shine on their mess.

4. To my mother I leave my veil, my wing, the window and time. I, artifact. In this age the hand is a voice.

5. I leave the voice, the wonder, the mirror, and my lens, bent and beholden to the worm, leaf-work in wrought iron, eerie illuminations and deep-sea vision.

6. I've seen the Eurostar, the drunken boat, and Davy Jones' Locker. I've seen Spanish galleons and the H. S. Mauberly covered in brine.

7. There is this line from cloud dander to the solo bulb of mourning, a string through common prayer.

8. I like it when the gray-green shadows suddenly dayglo over the rushes. The wind in my head.

9. To write is an equal and opposite reaction my comrade, communard, my friendo.

10. What is it finally thinking what in winter's dusty alcove, the body tocks. The day was cloudy. The light muddy, dreary when they took it down.

11. To Times Roman I give my stammer, my sullenness, my new world violence, form and all that, forms, and all that paper, gusts. Little buttress.

12. I send love and weapons to everyone possessed with night visions.

13. When those green lights flash and blink, is that it? When the "it" continues strangely for a bit, then falls into a line, is it over?

14. I quantified daily the wonder in the grain.

15. I found I was over and singular yet many, the many and the singular, the many and the evolutionary, the many in the grain. Many more.

16. Who in hell am I writing for?

17. This vision is silly, teenage, and mine, a spot on the negative, a hole in composition. I quantify, I loaf, I wonder, I find, I rev.

18. Here the days' mud, night is a satellite, and anger, my cleft, my birthmark and star.

19. Anger might be a better way to say "I love you," truer than "how are you in space"? Are you cold, can I get you a blanket?

20. To the polestar I leave my alien regalia, my off-world headdress. I leave acoustic forms in time, blooming, sudsy, inconsolable.

21. If you are unsatisfied, then welcome.

22. Here there are people working every corner of every inch of grass. The meticulously arranged outside reminds me of ocean and feels old.

23. In space the letterforms "I love" oscillate in waves.

24. I lose myself in waves speaking the half of me that forgot to say "goodbye" when I meant to say "how come."

25. Memory continues to bloom. More songs about death and dying, songs of inexperience.

26. More songs about being and loss, being in loss, more songs about seeing and feeling.

27. If you are critical, all the better to see and to miss it, to misunderstand, to fail at empathy and love, to not understand love and to love, to be diseverything and to love, whatever.

28. To mercy I leave whatever.

★

A Note on the Text

The good poets defy things
with their heart

This is how a fragment
enters the people

Don't say beauty say the beautiful
say the people

Say it is through chants that writing
entered the people

Their imagery and love of nature,
englutted flowers

This place of fleshlessness
Here is my song

the only recourse of sun
Even its smallest syllables

can be sown into the mouth
It is on the tongue the sun abides

Two syllables fastened
to each end

To stretch the vocal pattern
Its linenlike thread

True Discourse on Power

When I say the ghost has begun
you understand what is being said.
That time is not how we keep it
    or measure
first there was then wasn't . . .
It twitters and swerves like
    the evening news.
Now outside is 3D. Inside non-
    representational space.
Every law has an outside
    and inside
I have witnessed cruelty
break and gulp and sweat then
    punch out a smile.
To be awake. This talking in space.
To be absorbed in the ongoing.
Belief's a shadow to be looked into
    and into
until relief is gone. The dark
triangle settled in the midst of
    traffic is on us.
Time comes in adverbial bursts,
a glass of beer, a smoke . . .
The evening air refreshes, startles,

and the questions grow deeper like
          shadows across storefronts.
A forsythia ticking against
          the dirty pane.
This was time. Up. Down. Up.
And you were a part of it.
If I say it can you feel it now?
Imagine. Lightning strikes. Rain
          falls and drives.
Clouds pass. Night clarified. Stars.
In silent pictures the tree falls
          in the optic nerve.
The sound is chemistry.
There's no getting to it or if
          getting to it
feels like the actual sound
          is that silence?
Alone here with my shadows
          drawn . . .
So what's this about?
A horse and a castle, a tree
          and its leaving?
What's this about in solitary
          splendor?
The undertow and its threshold,
a door and the opening sky?

Or because a play of reflection
      lit up my bumper
and caught my eyes
I saw the shadow of a falcon.
Because a sound a poor man
      uttered
reached my ear I fell into song.
If the syntax of loyalty is not tragic
      then what is the wager?
If there were time, would it be ours?

Oversong

To be dark, to darken
to obscure, shade, dim

to tone down, to lower
overshadow, eclipse

to obfuscate, adumbrate
to cast into the shade

becloud, bedim, be-
darken, to cast a shadow

throw a shade, throw
a shadow, to doubt

to dusk, extinguish
to put out, blow out

to exit, veil, shroud
to murk, cloud, to jet

in darkness, Vesta
midnight, Hypnos

Thanatos, dead of night
sunless, dusky, pitch

starless, swart, tenebrous
inky, Erebus, Orpheus

vestral, twilit, sooty, blae ...

History Is Made at Night

Out of the old place and out of time
the present inches into view
into prospective blue
and what the colors apprehend
in the eye, in the head, here
revved and pounding night is
alive to such thinking. Alive
to cobalt and what is missing
here or never seen there.
An orchestral sort of life:
Then. There. Now. Here.
Music and the head's harvest sound
and this blend of dissonance this
love of silence and aught
watches you, sees you
negotiate the present intensities
in the world and its apostrophes.

11

The eras come as chemistry. Felt.
A magic-lantern moment
playing on the ceiling
between the beams' aurora.
A pinhole discovery like a comet
in a mirror. Its relative tail
of debris. Ice flashing for miles
in moonless cold.
Step back and look at it.
This evensong reflected
inside the flame. Give it back
it calls to the fire,
give me back my name.
The body's seal is broken.
The almighty static gone.
The lost leader of an old film,
score still ringing.
A long sigh across
evening's rasp and grackle.

I I I

Why have you flown?
Above me the blue
of leaves in shapes
of fierce animals.
Cars in the yards
make ugly sounds
and the animals
touching them smell bad.
I loved your dark feathers
loved the odd song
time and again.
The long black
strands of hair
your saddest tunes
could conjure.
And my body also
a commotion of sound
and form. Of tides.

IV

I too am many cries from truth
more guttural than piercing, more
muffled than distant. Gmail
invites me to "go visible."
Is being invisible not enough?
A kind of vow like poetry
burning the candle down.
Bring back the haloed reverie.
Music, retake the haughty
night sky. Its storied rays
its creak and croak
its raven's wing tonality.

v

Bring back the old names
Thoth and Anubis, Charon
and Mercury. Let rust
comfort the technoscape
troubling my interior.
A nesting doll consciousness
small and far away
opening each torn scene.
But what else is there
when so many are asleep
in this age of sand, yes, sand
in the eyes and in the heart.
It's hard to get a footing,
the mechanics are exhausting.

VI

Was it not troubling, sleep?
Was it not unmanageable, desire?
When happy no longer fit
the occasion. When unhappy
fit too well. Un happy.
What does it mean to not fight
to not break the spell
of sinking, sad fantast, wrong
turning in the mind.
Take it another way. Tune
the sad song and praise life.
Praise its contest of night and air.

VII

A broken patrician is a dangerous melody
in the high August night air.
A strange chromaticism
awaking the boy.
I begin my encampment here,
full throated by the stars
we sometimes muster
to some greater purpose,
greater summit. Maybe.
Step back and look at the picture.
It plays for a reason, mister,
people are nuts about it
and curious to pay for a glimpse
of that gaslit underworld.

VIII

I have always been awake
beneath glances, past
doorways, corridors.
I never see through you
but *through* you the joy
of all that is there anyway,
singing. The world
is rising and crashing,
a crescendo all the time.
Why not start
with the whole note?
Bring all you got,
show me that stuff.

I X

All my life this
jeweled perspective
thinking the night sky
as a boy would
keep me up
burning with adventure.
That the biology
that composes I
is shared with I.

X

So the lace and downy light
undoes me. Because looking
at your face here as it changes
the gemmed scene
I am also changing love.
For now let's consider
the world is good
and the night is rocket
or the colossus
of these festival sparks
falling now on us, all around us.
Even daylight is historic
if you think on it
if you really feel its cold rays,
old poetry, spreading evenly
over as far as you can see.

Bardo

I've spent my life
in a lone mechanical whine,

this combustion far off.

How fathomless to be
embedded in glacial ice,

what piece of self hiding there.

I am not sure about meaning
but understand the wave.

No more Novalis out loud.

No Juan de la Cruz singing
"I do not die to die."

No solstice, midhaven, *midi*, nor twilight.

No "isn't it amazing," no
none of that.

To crow, to crown, to cry, to crumble.

The trees the air warms into
a bright something

a bluish nothing into

clicks and pops
bursts and percussive runs.

I come with my asymmetries,
my untutored imagination.

Heathenish,

my homespun vision
sponsored by the winter sky.

Then someone said nether,
someone whirr.

And if I say the words
will you know them?

Is there world?
Are they still calling it that?

★

Modern Adventures at Sea

Say it then or
sing it out.
These voyages, waves.
The bluing of all I see.
Sing it with a harp
or tambourine.
With a drum and fiddle.
These notes and its staff,
the lines' tracery
blooming horizon.
These figures insisting.
Their laws. I embrace
accident. I accidentally
become a self in sun
in the middle of day.
Where are you? Cloud,
what shadow speaks
for me. I wonder.
Is there an end
to plastic. Is
yesterday the new
tomorrow. And
is that a future?
Do we get to

touch it and be
content here
before we go.
That the signs
won't remain
untranslatable
in the end.
And that I may
learn this language.
That there could
be a language
say with a dolphin,
a dog, a cattle herder
and slaughterhouse,
a lumberyard
and big redwood.
That someone
could say to the crude.
Stay there. And
don't be drawn
into this tired game.
I wonder if the poem
gets tired. If
the song is worn
like sea glass.
I wonder if I am
up to this light.

These ideas of order
and all I feel
walking down
the avenue.
I see the sap
weeping on the cars.
See the wrack
about my feet.
Its state of decay.
To see that decay
as the best of all
worlds before me.
It's transformation
not transportation
that's needed. Here.
It's embracing
the soft matter
running my engine.
My guff. And fright.
This piss and
vinegar. And tears.
That I won't
commit violence
to myself in mind.
Or to others
with cruel words.
That I may break

this chain-link ism
of bigger than
smaller than why
feel bigger than
anyone feeling smaller.
Can I transform
this body
I steward. This
my biomass.
My accident.
When lost at sea
I found a voice,
alive and cresting,
crashing, falling
and rising. To drift,
digress, to dream
of the voice. Its
grain. To feel
its vibrations. Pitch.
Its plural noises.
To be upheld
in it, to love.
Whose book lying
on that table?
And where does
the voice
come from?

What life
was attached
to its lift,
to its feint,
its gift of sight.
To understand
oneself. With-
out oneself.
How to live.
What to do.

ACKNOWLEDGEMENTS: Some poems, often in different versions, appeared in these journals: *The Baffler, Boundary 2, The Brooklyn Rail, The Cambridge Literary Review, Colorado Review, Conjunctions, Critical Review, Fence, Friends, GlitterPony, Hambone, Jubilat, The Literary Review, The Nation, Poetry, Skein,* and *The Small Caps Anthology.* Some poems were included in the limited-edition book *In Song & Story* (Amsterdam: Tungsten, 2010); the chapbooks *Pinocchio's Gnosis* (Northampton: Song Cave, 2011) and *History Is Made at Night* (Cincinnati: Students of Decay, 2011); the folio *Tiny Blast* (Boulder: Kavyayantra Press, 2009) and the broadside "Basement Song" (Amsterdam: Tungsten, 2010). A few lines from these poems are part of the film-poem *Threshold Songs* by Natalia Almada & Peter Gizzi (Paris & Tangier: Tamaas, 2010). My thanks to all involved. Many thanks to the good people at the University of Massachusetts, Amherst for affording me leave time, at Yaddo for a month in 2009, and at Cambridge University for a fellowship from January to August of 2011. To the many individuals who have made valuable comments I express my deepest thanks, and especially to Elizabeth Willis, always.

PETER GIZZI is the author of *The Outernationale, Some Values of Landscape and Weather, Artificial Heart*, and *Periplum*. He has also published several limited-edition chapbooks, folios, and artist books. His honors include the Lavan Younger Poet Award from the Academy of American Poets, and fellowships in poetry from The Howard Foundation, The Foundation for Contemporary Arts, and The John Simon Guggenheim Memorial Foundation; in 2011 he was the Judith E. Wilson Visiting Fellow in Poetry at Cambridge University. His editing projects have included *o•blék: a journal of language arts, The Exact Change Yearbook, The House That Jack Built: The Collected Lectures of Jack Spicer*, and, with Kevin Killian, *My Vocabulary Did This to Me: The Collected Poetry of Jack Spicer*; from 2008 to 2011 he was the poetry editor for *The Nation*. He works at the University of Massachusetts, Amherst.

DATE DUE